BECOMING

A

PROFESSIONAL

Joanne Griffiths

BECOMING

A

PROFESSIONAL

YTC Press

Monograph Series

YTC Press

An imprint dedicated to research on Youth, Theology & Culture

First published in 2007 by

YTC Press

– A Division of Youth Focus –

www.ytcpress.com

www.youthfocus.biz

ISBN: 978-1-84753-720-1

Youth Focus

Youth Focus is a partnership dedicated to providing good quality resources for those involved in Christian youth ministry at an affordable price. We undertake this ministry by

- Training volunteer, part-time and full-time youth workers throughout the world through our accredited online Emerge Academy, www.emergeacademy.net
- Providing lecture resources (scripts, handouts and PowerPoint presentations) for those involved in teaching youth ministry and associated disciplines, www.youthfocus.biz
- Publishing books, with our YTC Imprint through www.lulu.com, on youth ministry, ecclesiology, cultural studies, theology, education and associated disciplines

Youth Focus is based in the UK but partners with organisations around the world.

For more information, please contact Steve Griffiths through steve@youthfocus.biz or go to the websites:

www.youthfocus.biz
www.emergeacademy.net
www.ytcpress.com

This book is dedicated to the students of Centre for Youth Ministry, Cambridge.

Also for Steve, Scott, Lee and Rebekah

Contents

Acknowledgments

I would like to thank Dr Simon Bradford from Brunel University for his unending support, guidance, helpful comments and, above all, encouragement during the course of this study.

My thanks go to Evie Xinos at Brunel University who provided helpful administration support when I needed it.

I am grateful to my colleagues at Cambridge Centre for Youth Ministry who provided much sympathy, cups of tea, lots of encouragement and helpful discussions about my topic.

I have appreciated the support of my husband Steve who has walked this study path with me. He is my constant friend and encourager and I am more grateful to him than he will ever know.

My three children, Scott, Lee and Rebekah, thank you. You have endured me working evenings and weekends for too long now. Thank you for understanding and maintaining your sense of humour throughout it all.

I would like to thank my parents, Morris and Vennie and my in-laws, Frank and Doreen for encouraging me the whole way through.

Finally, I would like to thank the thirty-three participants who so willingly took part in this study. Their generosity of time, within very busy lives, was humbling. It was a privilege to have spent time with youth workers who are genuinely committed to young people and the profession. Thank you.

Chapter One

Introduction

The subject under investigation is the professional socialisation of graduating youth workers from a full-time degree course into full-time employment. This research arises from my own training and working life in three ways. First, I am a tutor on a full-time degree course for Christian youth workers. Second, I have been involved in youth work for twenty years, both as a volunteer and in full-time employment. Third, I graduated from the course on which I now tutor five years ago and have undergone the very process that I am researching.

Defining Youth Work

The National Youth Agency (NYA) describes the main purpose of youth work as, "the personal and social development of young people and their social inclusion" (NYA: np). They define youth work as helping young people, usually between the ages of 13 and 19, to learn about themselves, others and society through non-formal educational activities as opposed to formal or compulsory education. Youth work should take a holistic approach, encompassing intellectual, physical, emotional and spiritual aspects of a young persons wellbeing and development (NYA: 2007). This is the definition of youth work that will be used within this study.

According to Carpenter & Platt (1997:339), professionalism implies a shared mission, purpose, goal, code of ethics, value system and a sense of unity and association. If youth work is regarded in the light of this definition, then it most certainly is a profession. The shared mission, purpose and goal can be derived from the definition of youth work above. There is now an ethical conduct in youth work (NYA:2004) that guides youth workers on how to practice ethically within the profession. The value system and sense of unity and association are those issues that the youth worker develops throughout their training and into their careers.

The amount of avenues for professional training for youth workers is growing, with the JNC (Joint Negotiating Committee) providing the professional qualification with which to enter full-time work.

Centre for Youth Ministry

The Centre for Youth Ministry (CYM), founded ten years ago to address the lack of professional full-time training for Christian youth workers in Britain, is a consortium of training and youth work agencies providing courses, research and resources into Christian youth work. The full-time BA (Hons) Degree in Youth and Community Work with Applied Theology is validated by Oxford Brookes University and endorsed by the NYA. This course, delivered in five Regional Centres (London, Oxford, Nottingham, Bristol and Cambridge) confers a JNC qualification after two years and a degree after three years study. CYM will be referred to often within this book as it forms a crucial part of the context.

Overview of Chapters

Chapter Two reviews the literature that is relevant to the research. Here, a definition for 'professional socialisation' will be provided, leading to a review of the research that provides an overview of the issues affecting individuals during the professional socialisation phase. The work of Fred Davis (1968) will be explored in some detail in order to provide an understanding of the phases of transition. The wider context is explored through a consideration of career and organisational socialisation. Finally, literature relevant to professional socialisation and professional identity will be considered.

Methodology is outlined in Chapter Three. The overall research strategy of case study was used, with focus groups, questionnaires and semi-structured interviews implemented as the data collection tools. The effectiveness of these methods is discussed within the chapter, as are the selection of the participants and ethical issues involved, alongside a reflection on my role as researcher.

The main findings form the basis of Chapter Four, exploring the clear transitional phase for youth workers during the professional socialisation period. The key findings were

- impact of the course on learning and development
- feelings that youth workers begin their first post with

- expectations that youth workers have about the profession once graduated

- impressions that youth workers form about what is expected of them

- a desire to perform well within the first post

- integration of knowledge and learning within the new post

- a strong sense of professional identity and

- the importance of support structures within the professional socialisation phase and continuing professional development.

In Chapter Five, I interpret these findings in light of the literature previously reviewed. The six stages of Davis will provide a framework for this chapter, that of;

1) *Initial Innocence*, the beginning of the first post when feelings of nervousness and worry dominate;

2) *Labelled recognition of Incongruity* when youth workers may question their chosen profession;

3) *Psyching out*, when youth workers try to 'work out' how to perform well in their post;

4) *Role simulation*, when youth workers perform what they 'think' is the accepted behaviour of a professional youth worker;

5) *Provisional Internalization*, when the youth worker tries to integrate his or her learning into the new role in a more genuine way, but they still regress back to old ways at times;

6) *Stable Internalization*, when the youth workers' professional identity is strong and secure but is open to continuous development.

7) Finally, there is a seventh point, that of *Support Structures*. Although not found in the Davis study, it was a key finding within the research and therefore warrants inclusion.

Conclusions are presented in Chapter Six. Here, implications for the profession of youth work are provided alongside implications for both CYM and the graduating youth worker. Opportunities for further study are also explored.

Chapter Two

Literature Review

In reviewing the literature used to inform my study, I acknowledge that the predominant source is that of other disciplines; mainly medical, teaching and social work. There has, to date, been little research generated around the subject of professional socialisation within the field of youth work. First, I will provide a definition of professional socialisation. Second I will provide an overview of professional socialisation in various contexts. Third, I will consider the literature that focuses on the transitional stages that occur during professional socialisation. Fourth, I will consider the concept of micro-socialisation. Fifth, I will discuss the impact of organisational socialisation. Finally, I will consider professional identity in the light of professional socialisation.

Defining Professional Socialisation

Key theorist Erik Erikson (1950) spoke at length about the socialisation process in his study on the eight stages of man, where he described personality development from infancy to adulthood. Erikson suggested that an individual must complete each stage satisfactorily in order to progress to the next stage. If that does not happen, psychological development will be hampered, causing problems in later life. Abercrombie, Hill and Turner (1984) understand socialisation to be, "the process whereby people learn to conform to social norms" (1984:201). They have placed Erikson's eight stages into three broader stages. The primary stage involves the socialisation of young children in the family. The secondary stage relates to schooling whilst the third stage relates to adult socialisation, in which roles such as parent, husband, wife or employee are practiced (1984). It is the third stage that relates to this study – the notion of professional socialisation, rooted in the broader socialisation context.

Gillespie (1995) offers a basic definition of professional socialisation as, "the process by which people selectively acquire the values, attitudes, interests, skills, knowledge and culture current in the groups of which they are or seek to become a member" (1995:122). Jacox (1973) and Cohen (1981), cited in Adams *et al* 2006, provide a further definition that acknowledges the impact on professional identity:

> Professional socialization is the complex process by which a person acquires the knowledge, skills, and sense of occupational identity that are characteristic of a member of that profession. It involves the internalization of the values and norms of the group into the person's own behaviour and self-conception. (Jacox 1973; Cohen 1981:14, cited in Adams *et al* 2006)

I view professional socialisation within youth work to be the process of change that trainee youth workers experience when undertaking a full-time course. They commence studies as a layperson and, over a period of three years, re-form into a professional. This process includes the formation of a professional identity.

Professional Socialisation – an overview

Countless pieces of research within medicine and teaching have explored the professional socialisation processes of students. Caires and Almeida (2005), for example, found that the two hundred trainee teachers in their Portuguese study experienced significant changes, as a consequence of professional socialisation, within the areas of learning and professional development. The organisational culture of student placements also had an impact on the student. The course was five years long; four years of theoretical study with the final year being in a placement school. The study found that student confidence was raised, they considered themselves to be 'professional' in their practice and attitudes, and many spoke of facing a 'personal revolution' (2005:116). Similarly, this could easily describe the changes that students experience during the CYM course. The research I have conducted suggests a dramatic change in the views and practices of the youth workers who have completed the course, starting from when they begin the course and continuing long after graduation. This will be discussed at more length later in Chapter Five.

Those wishing to join CYM must have previous youth work experience to be accepted onto the course. This contrasts with Caires and Almeida, whose students began their studies with limited experience. My study suggests that youth work students have already undergone certain processes relating to past experiences that will have had an impact on their professional development before starting the course. Whilst Caires and Almeida do not provide adequate exploration of the impact of prior professional knowledge on a student, the work of Robson (1998) sheds some light on this area. Robson (1998) conducted an ethnographic case study researching the transitional experiences of a student Further Education (FE) teacher during a course that consisted of both theory and practice. The research provides interesting insights into the transitions experienced. Interviewed at various stages throughout the twelve-month duration of the course, teaching practice was focused on as a key area of change. The participant reflected on her progression, with specific regard to the development of her own teaching style rather than the copying of styles that she had experienced as a young person in college. The participant actively explored her role in relation to students, teaching staff in her placement and college tutors. Each of these roles required something different from her and this was stressful at times. By focussing on how the past professional experience of the subject impacted her new role, Robson noted both the complication and enrichment of the professional socialisation process.

The participants in my study have all had previous employment experience; usually a combination of a full-time job and voluntary youth work. Analysis of the data suggests that there is a link between past experiences and the choice of their first full-time youth work post.

Having considered studies that provide an overview of the effects of professional socialisation, we now turn to the process of professional socialisation.

Transitional Stages

Davis *et al* (1968) cited in Becker *et al Institutions and the Person: Papers Presented to Everett C. Hughes*, conducted a five-year longitudinal study of student nurses in the United States. Davis' study focused on the interaction between lay and professional cultures during the learning period and discussed 'doctrinal conversion'; the consequence of the process whereby students internalise the teaching and culture of nursing. Although conducted in 1968, the transitionary phase for students still remains despite changes within nursing education. Davis defines six stages of progression.

> The process consists of six successive stages: (1) Initial Innocence, (2) Labeled Recognition of Incongruity, (3) "Psyching Out," (4) Role Simulation, (5) Provisional Internalization, and (6) Stable Internalization. (Davis 1968:241)

Initial Innocence is characterized by a strong lay imagery of the profession that students bring with them when they embark on a course. This period is dominated by feelings of self-doubt, worry and frustration, with students feeling they need to perform in the way they think is expected of them.

Labeled Recognition of Incongruity, probably the most difficult time for students, is when they begin to question their choice of profession and may seek out other alternatives. This is often due to the fact that their expectations about the profession are very different from those being taught by the faculty.

Psyching Out involves students 'working out' how to impress their tutors. They realise what tutors expect of them and actively work to satisfy these expectations. Whilst some students display this stage early on, it does not come to pass until the second stage has been achieved.

Role Simulation is what Davis refers to as, "the performance implementation of 'psyching out'"(1968:246), when the student is self-conscious and unsure of how to behave. This is often accompanied by feelings of guilt and hypocrisy, the student feeling they are merely 'play acting' the role of their chosen profession. Although the student may feel like this, others will view him or her as "trustworthy, competent and legitimate" (1968:247). In other words, the student is portraying what his or her performance is claiming to be (Davis 1968).

Provisional Internalization involves the student experiencing a recurrent failure to integrate the various areas of their learning. They may find it difficult, for example, to make connections between newly acquired knowledge and practice. Seeking commitment to the new profession, they are still loosely attached to the past and their old patterns of thought (Davis, 1968).

Davis regards *Stable Internalization* as the final part of doctrinal conversion. Despite occasional misgivings, the self-image is predominantly that of 'professional'. The student is now at ease talking about their performance and their professional identity has been formed by subjective means (Davis, 1968). They have become socialized into their profession by the way they have been taught; what Davis regards as 'doctrinal conversion'.

These stages are useful for the purposes of this study since they provide an understanding around the subjective issues involved in the processes of professional socialization. Interestingly, Davis concludes his work by noting that, once students are away from the teaching environment, they may revise, transform or regress in their professional identity. He states,

> It would be futile, however to speculate further on this question, inasmuch as our data thus far barely touch on the post-graduation phases of the students' careers. (Davis 1968:235)

This is the very stage that my study seeks to understand. Focussing on the post-graduation phase, I will be interacting with the Davis theory in order to determine a relationship between the subjective processes of professional socialization for both a student and a postgraduate. The indicators from the data collected suggest a correlation between the stages offered by Davis and the processes graduating youth workers experience in their first posts. Crucially, I am suggesting that the stages towards doctrinal conversion repeat themselves once graduates are within a new environment. Armed with the knowledge and skills of their profession, they do not have to re-learn 'youth work'. However, they do have to learn their new role as a qualified professional youth worker and all the expectations that entails.

Becker *et al* (1961) recognized the common experience of professional training amongst many young people. This observation from 1961 is just as true today, especially for the field of youth work, which attracts many under-25s as a career of choice. Becker *et al* considered that, although these young people may be married with families and other 'adult' responsibilities, they enter a period of professional adolescence upon completion of their training during which they need to show adult competence and learning without being given full adult responsibility. It is this professionally adolescent period that will be considered within this study.

Career Socialisation

Corcoran and Clark (1984) illuminate the processes of professional socialisation further. In their study, "Professional Socialisation and Contemporary Career Attitudes of Three University Faculty Generations" (1984:131), career socialisation and entry into occupations was discussed. They conceived a three-stage model depicting the forming of adult occupational identity (1984:133). The first stage, "anticipatory socialisation" (1984:133), describes the pre-entry stage of the chosen career. It "includes the process by which persons choose occupations and are recruited to them, gradually taking on the values of the group to which they aspire" (1984:133). The second stage includes, or is preceded by, formal schooling for the occupation. For faculty members, this is an intensive time that provides, "anticipatory socialisation, a site for recruitment, and through interactions, the facilitation of professional role commitment" (1984:135). If all goes well, the third stage is achieved and sees a continuation of the role to which the trainee has aspired. He or she will have "internalized role specifications" (1984:135) and will have achieved a high degree of job satisfaction, involvement and commitment (Corcoran and Clark, 1984). The career route, however, may be unstable due to difficulties within the organisation. This may intrude on the levels of success for the new worker. This work is applicable to my study because it provides a simple model of socialisation focusing on 'career'.

Corcoran and Clark's (1984) third stage of career socialization develops further Davis' notion of Stable Internalization, noting how the individual matures and has internalized roles (1984:135). Corcoran and Clark's role continuance has a sense of longevity attached to it that is missing from the Davis stages. In developing this, they comment on the high degree of job commitment and involvement of the professional. He or she becomes more independent, perhaps taking on leadership roles. If the career route is unstable in any way, though, problems may occur. Again, these issues will be more fully discussed in Chapter Five.

Organisational Socialisation

Entry into an organisation is the beginning of a specific socialisation (Nicholson 1996). Nicholson expands on the definition of organizational socialisation by saying, "professional organisations operate to ensure that new members are aware of the rules and values that ensure the perpetuation of the dominant culture of that organisation and group" (1996:71). With this explanation in mind, students experience a period of organisational socialisation after graduation and initial embarkation on their first post.

This process continues throughout the career (Erikson, 1950; Becker, 1964; Brim, 1966, cited in Corcoran and Clark). Newly qualified youth workers may find that the initial period in a new post can be either a supportive, relatively stress free time or an unsupportive, confusing and isolating period, depending on the organisation they find themselves working within. Hayon and Ben-Peretz (1986) undertook qualitative research of newly qualified teachers on the concerns they face upon starting a full-time teaching post after leaving university. The organisation chosen by graduates made a tangible difference to the success of their socialisation period.

Clearly, a new working environment can place strain during socialisation, as noted in the study of Prince *et al* (2000). This qualitative research on undergraduate medical students' perceptions and attitudes towards their transition from theoretical to clinical training has much to say around the subject of professional socialisation. The results suggested that students had difficulty in bridging the gap between the theoretical and clinical phase of the curriculum. The problems they experienced arose largely from professional socialisation processes, such as long working hours and problems adjusting to a new working environment.

Support Structures

The issues raised relating to a new working environment are also explored in the research of Jones (2005). From this, a key finding was the use of support structures for new teachers. Jones used a case study approach and conducted semi-structured questionnaires and interviews with ten newly qualified teachers (NQTs), all of whom had completed a Post Graduate Certificate in Education (PGCE). One of the aspects Jones researched was how new teachers managed the socialisation process. Jones found that one of the most important aspects for NQTs was being able to talk to other teachers, sharing experiences and worries. The distinction between professional and personal was explored with Jones explaining about one of the research participants who resigned from teaching after the first year:

> ...where the personal dimension of induction to be measured in the quality of the relationship established between the new teacher, the induction tutor and other colleagues had been neglected, newly qualified teachers' emotional and physical welfare was affected (Jones 2005:523).

It is interesting that these 'non-taught' aspects of professional socialization should come to the fore once in a new post. Indeed, much of Jones' research found that the 'non-taught' issues for students dominated the professional socialization phase. Jones also explored the culture of the school where the NQT was based. Youth work posts are usually more isolating than teaching posts, especially within a church context that may not have an adequate management structure in place.

This 'non-taught' aspect of professional socialization is discussed further through the research of Moon *et al* (2000), focusing on the education of teachers, who identified the use of student cohorts as a vehicle of intensifying the socialisation experience. Suggesting that, "most professional schools have mechanisms to educate and socialise students into a given field" (2000:739), they go on to say that there is a "hidden curriculum" (2000:739) involved in the formal training of professionals that "helps enculturate students into the norms of a profession" (2000:739). Moon *et al* did not define what the hidden curriculum was. This would strongly link with the Jones research and the 'non-taught' aspects of the course.

The lack of clarification around the hidden curriculum and 'non-taught' aspects of the course has provided an area to explore within this dissertation. Youth workers learn a significant amount from informal factors, such as conversations with colleagues and friends, which help to socialise them into the profession. Indeed, insights into the data collected shows that the participants viewed the social interaction between themselves, college peer group and tutors to have been highly valuable during the training experience. Participants told of how they missed the friendship of their fellow students once they left the course, highlighting an important 'non-taught' aspect of the course. One youth worker even described his fellow students and tutors as a 'family'. The participants of my study did not specifically identify these informal structures as being significant to their learning but it is precisely these structures that had much bearing on the formation of the students. Being able to reflect and discuss their practice in less formal ways, and having an informal support structure that energised the students, was considered an important part of the course. This is a key issue to explore within this study. As youth workers are informal educators, the importance of informal mechanisms within the training period of a formal course has significant implications for future course delivery.

Micro-socialisation

Fidler and Atton (2003) conducted research amongst head teachers and the challenges they face in contemporary schooling. Professional socialisation for head teachers was discussed at length within this research. Head teachers found that professional and organisational socialisation was a cause for concern for them, since many head teachers move to a new and unfamiliar school, which they must get to know and understand. Head teachers, professionally trained and already socialised into the teaching profession, must then embark on a process of, "socialisation for leadership and management" (Hart and Weindling 1996, cited in Fidler and Atton 2003:153). This introduces 'micro-socialisation', the notion that an individual broadly socialised into a profession will have a further period of socialisation when there is a radical change in role.

The participants within this study have been doing youth work in some form for many years. Therefore, they too will have experienced this concept of 'micro-socialisation'. This raises important issues too for those who have been volunteers or part-time youth workers in that they will have experienced major changes, especially in terms of their expectations of professional youth work. Adams *et al* (2006) remark how there may be an, "idealized version of a profession, as portrayed *to* novice professionals, and the real work practised *by* the existing members of the profession" (Melia: 1987 cited in Adams *et al*

2006:57). It is these idealized concepts of a profession, referred to by Davis in his doctrinal conversion stages, which can cause so much discomfort for a student. This could also be related to the newly qualified youth worker undertaking a new role. The consequences on the professional identity of the youth worker need to be considered next.

Professional Identity

The process by which professional identity forms and develops does not proceed in a linear way (Niema: 1997, cited in Adams *et al* (2006). Professional socialisation is ultimately about change – and how individuals cope with that change. Marshal *et al* (2001) see change as being, "intimately connected with a sense of identity" (2001:189). In similar vein, Erikson commented that, "identity is never gained nor maintained once and for all" (1950:57). Adams *et al* (2006) view professional identity as something that develops over time and involves the gaining of insights into professional practices. This leads to the development of talents and values of the profession (Adams *et al*: 2006). There is a relationship between professional socialisation and professional identity that I cannot ignore. Payne (2004) comments on how professional identity is under constant negotiation within workplaces and organisations. He continues to say that managerial responsibilities have been particularly influential on professional identity (2004:5). The work of Wenger (1998), in his study of 'practice communities', develops insight into multi-disciplinary teams and views the working within these teams to affect the professional roles and identities of these teams. This has particular relevance to the youth work profession in the current political climate. With the introduction of *Every Child Matters* and the implementation of Children's Trusts across the country, multi-disciplinary teams will be central to the delivery of services for children and young people. The professional identity of youth workers will be in constant flux so successful socialisation into the profession is more important than ever. My research suggests that the professional identity of the participants is a direct response to the socialisation of those participants into the youth work profession. Although most of the participants had begun to form their professional identity before starting the course, the findings suggest that the CYM course had a strong influence on their professional identity. Therefore, another key point to explore within this study is the impact of professional socialisation on the professional identity of graduating youth workers.

Conclusion

Well-equipped and confident youth workers can make a profound difference to young people, their communities and society. Taking into account the writers within this literature review, when they express the difficulties people face during professional socialisation, it is clear that graduates need to be prepared as much as possible for their first job on leaving the course. This period of change and transition within the profession could be a time of great stress for the individual:

> During the most crucial periods of any career, a man suffers greater psychological stress than during other periods. This is perhaps less so if he is not aware of his opportunities and dangers...but probably it is more usual to be aware, or to be made so by colleagues and seniors, of the nature of imminent or current crises. (Becker, S & Strauss, A 1956:253)

This study enables me to provide students with information that will raise their awareness of the opportunities and dangers, referred to by Becker and Strauss, which they could experience during the transitional phases of their careers.

This literature has raised a number of key areas. First, there is the notion that changes occur for youth workers upon entering and exiting the course. Second, we note the importance of micro-socialisation and the impact that a change of role within the profession has on youth workers. Third, there is the issue of informal and formal aspects of professional socialisation, focusing particularly on the 'non-taught' aspects of the course. Fourth, the stages of doctrinal conversion and the notion of professional socialisation being a subjective process as noted in the study of Davis (1968) are of special importance. Fifth, the impact of support structures greatly impacts on youth workers during times of change. Sixth, the employing organisation has a significant impact. Finally, we are minded to consider how professional identity is impacted during professional socialisation.

Chapter Three

Methodology

> The…researcher is not only intimately and autobiographically related to the question but learns to love the question. It becomes a kind of song into which the researcher breathes life not only because the question leads to an answer, but also because the question itself is infused in the researcher's being. It creates a thirst to discover, to clarify, and to understand crucial dimensions of knowledge and experience. (Moustakas, 1990:43)

This research project is ultimately about how Christian youth workers construct meaning and self-understanding from the working environment in which find themselves once graduated and how their learning and beliefs, developed during a vocational youth work and applied theology degree course, have impacted this experience. In order to provide a logical framework for the research process, this chapter will explain the focus and design of the study, selection of the participants, description of research methods used, ethical issues involved in the study, my role as researcher and data collection tools used.

The focus of this inquiry and the methods used to research the question are highly compatible with a qualitative social science based approach.

> Whether dealing with meanings or with patterns of behaviour, qualitative researchers tend to rely on a detailed and intricate description of events or people. (Denscombe 2000:175)

Heath reiterates this,

> Qualitative researchers attempt to describe and interpret some human phenomenon, often in the words of selected individuals. (Heath 1997: np)

The research arises from my belief that professional identity for Christian youth workers takes on a new meaning once they take up their first full-time position. As this is essentially a period of transition for the youth worker, this research can be described as a 'phenomenological inquiry'. Phenomenology seeks to get underneath in order to describe and understand the meanings behind human experience. Moustakas (1994) labels this kind of inquiry 'heuristic research'. This means to 'discover' or 'to find' (Moustakas, quoted in Newton and Rudestam 2001:38). A question is sought at the beginning of the research that the researcher wants to answer in a personally meaningful way to understand the relationship between oneself and the world. This also has social significance that can include stories and dialogue as sources of data (Rudestam and Newton 2001:39). This study has resonance with the values of heuristic research by exploring the relationship between the youth worker and their new professional world. The aim of the research is to examine the sociological issues that impact on graduating youth workers as they make the transition from student to professional employee. In addition, the phenomenon of the professional transition is analysed by using the stories and experiences of past students from the CYM course, all have experienced first hand the process that is being researched.

A case study approach was an appropriate strategy to adopt, enabling a range of research methods to be used. Denscombe (2000) discusses five elements that provide a researcher with a rationale for undertaking a case study approach.

1. *Spotlight on one instance.* This is the starting point and in this research study the one instance being explored was, as already mentioned, the transition experienced when students become employees. The logic behind looking at one case instead of many is that insights can be gained by examining the particular case (Denscombe 2000:30).

2. *In-depth study.* A case study approach has enabled me to investigate in detail and discover insights that may not have been otherwise apparent. I wanted to investigate the detail of the transition period and a case study allowed me to do this mainly by using a variety of research methods.

3. *Focus on relationships and processes.* This is a key area of the research. The case study approach, according to Denscombe, can deal with a case as a whole and can discover how various parts of the whole affect one another (Denscombe 2000:31). Indeed, this relates well to Moustakas' (1994) idea of heuristic research as noted earlier since the case study approach seeks to explain 'why' certain outcomes may happen. Investigating the processes around post-graduation identity construction will provide an in-depth and exciting insight of real benefit to the wider field.

4. *Natural setting.* This is based on the understanding that the case being studied already exists and will continue to exist after the research.

The research design will not impose controls on variables, but the case study will research the variables as they are, in order to measure a 'naturally occurring phenomenon' (Yin 1994: quoted in Denscombe 2000:31). The research should not adversely affect any of the experiences being investigated. Indeed, the process being studied will continue to exist as long as youth workers continue to undertake professional training and seek employment within the field after graduating.

5. *Multiple sources and multiple methods.* Case study allows for a variety of research methods. A combination of focus groups, questionnaires and interviews was used in this study. The purpose of the design was to enable the gathering of data in a progressive manner, that is, each method provided a richer and more in-depth source of data. The data from the focus groups raised the issues that needed to be addressed in the questionnaires. The questionnaires provided a 'snap shot' of the issues that youth workers had faced. This, then, formed the framework for the semi-structured interviews. Finally, the semi-structured interviews provided an in-depth source of data, which could be critically analysed in light of wider reading.

The inherent weaknesses of a case study approach – credibility of generalizations made from its findings, the perceived production of 'soft' data (Denscombe 2000:40) and lack of control over variables (Richards 2005:20) – are more than offset by the strengths that the approach offers. These include the opportunity to investigate a complex situation, which offers a holistic analysis, rather than focusing on isolated factors. Attention to the particular and specific (Richards 2005:20) is enabled through a case study approach and in this study, the understandings of actual youth workers and their professional identity are explored. More importantly, the case study approach and the use of multi-methods enhance the validity of the data collected. The use of multi-methods allows for an investigation of the transition period of youth workers into full-time employment from different angles. The more data I collect, the more likely it is to improve the quality of the research (Denscombe 2000:84). This does not mean that the data analysis is necessarily absolutely 'right' but it does provide confidence if the meaning of the data collected from the focus groups, questionnaires and interviews together shows some consistency. Also, validity and reliability are strengthened if the findings are not too closely connected with one particular research method (Denscombe 2000:85).

Selection of Participants

Being a tutor on the course in Cambridge, it was not difficult for me to identify potential participants via the CYM database, which contained contact details and the first posts that were undertaken upon students graduating. I wanted to collect the views of those youth workers who had completed the full three years of the degree course at Cambridge as they had experienced the entire course rather than the first two years in which students had a choice to leave after gaining the JNC qualification. I assumed early on in the research-design that the third year could be a key time to explore since students would be deciding on future posts. It is also a time when students reflect on all they have learnt during the first two years. I wanted the participants to reflect the diverse nature of the field of youth work or, at the very least, my perceptions of the diverse nature of the field. Therefore, the participants chosen represented a varied range of youth work situations. From the database, graduates were identified who went to work for Christian and secular charities, churches (any denomination) and local authorities. There was one aspect of the research that involved a group of third-year students who were nearing their graduation and therefore did not fulfil the criteria entirely. This was a focus group and I wanted to hear about their hopes and fears for the future, as this would enable me to create appropriate questions for the questionnaires.

Thirty-three participants took part in the research. The actual distribution of participants is shown in brackets below. Only two participants had more than one of the characteristics identified below;

- More men than women (21:12). This is not a reflection of the gender balance at CYM, which is fairly evenly mixed across the year groups.
- Those working for Churches, any denomination (17)
- Those working for secular charities (5)
- Those working for Christian charities (5)
- Those working for Local Authority Youth Service (6)
- Majority white (31), minority black (2). This reflects the ethnic mix of CYM Cambridge, which draws a mainly white middle class group.

I recruited the participants for the research by emailing and phoning. An invitational letter was sent, which informed them about the aims of the research, the commitment expected and their rights when participating in a study. As there were various methods used within the research design, participants were identified gradually for each purpose but the same recruitment criteria for the focus groups (apart from the third-year student group), questionnaires and interviews were used.

Research Methods and Data Collection Tools

Focus Groups

Before devising the questionnaires, it was necessary to know what issues would be relevant to the study. In order to achieve this, two focus groups were conducted; one with a group of past graduates and one with the current third-year group who were nearing the end of the course and looking for jobs. The rationale for the two groups was that one group could discuss what the issues were once they had graduated and one group could discuss their hopes and fears for the future. This would inform my thinking when devising the questions for the questionnaires. As the researcher, I became more a facilitator than interviewer (Bell, 2005). I chose to take a semi-structured approach, with six questions. These were intended to keep the group focused on the issues I wanted discussed. Both interviews were recorded and transcribed.

The first group conducted was the postgraduate group. All five members knew each other, as they had studied together. There was an instant rapport within the group that throughout the time was a disadvantage, as I had to work hard at keeping the group focused. However, there was also a deeper level of openness that occurred within the discussions, as they spoke openly about some difficult experiences they had when they left the course and started their first posts.

The second group consisted of the third-year students, nearing completion of the course. Members of this group were well known to each other, therefore conversation was lively and fast moving. Fortunately, the group kept focused on the topic to be discussed, as they were extremely interested in the research area. I gained a richer understanding of the fears that students faced upon finishing their training. A question asked was, "do you feel ready to take on any type of youth work post be it in a Christian or secular setting?" This provided a range of answers, rooted in whatever fieldwork context they had undertaken whilst on the course. This focus group enabled me to develop questions based around fears and anxieties that graduates may experience.

Questionnaires

Thirteen structured questionnaires were completed and returned from a distribution of thirty-five. These reflected a diverse sample of graduates, working in churches, Christian charities, secular charities and local authorities. The use of questionnaires was chosen for several reasons.

First, this was a practical method that could be implemented using email to reach youth workers who were spread across the UK. Once graduated, the newly qualified youth workers had undertaken posts throughout the country so trying to gather thirty-five of the graduates together for focus groups or interviews would have been extremely difficult and costly. It was also practical for the participants in that they completed a questionnaire within a three-week deadline. The questionnaire was emailed, enabling the participants to complete it and simply email it back. This was convenient for both participants and me.

Second, questionnaires provided data about thoughts and feelings that were experienced. Of course, the questionnaire would not have been a sufficient method, in and of itself, to gain a real understanding of the issues being raised. Follow-up or probing questions were not possible and the interviews allowed for a more in-depth approach towards gaining data that would provide greater validity.

Third, the use of questionnaires provided consistency of structure for each participant. The data from the questionnaires provided a framework and direction for the next step of the research, the semi-structured interviews.

Semi-structured Interviews

This method provided more in-depth data. All interviewees were asked the same core questions. However, the semi-structured interview method meant that when the opportunity arose, deeper questions could be asked. These took the form of probing, follow-up or clarification questions.

On a practical level, conducting the interviews was a very time consuming process. Ten people were interviewed, all living and working in various locations around London and Cambridge. Contacting and making dates to interview the participants was the most frustrating element of the research. All the participants were incredibly busy people. This meant the interviews had to be conducted across a number of weeks. All those interviewed had graduated throughout the last five years. The strength of this provided me with an insight into developments and changes that may have occurred within the course and the impact this had on the students graduating. As a researcher, I was keen to hear the stories of these participants and the interviews were particularly useful in enabling stories to emerge. Indeed, Brunner (1990) argues that 'meaning-making' is embedded within stories and that people achieve meaning through shared encounters, including the telling of their stories. As it was these meanings I wanted to investigate, the interviews provided an excellent opportunity in which to explore with the participants further.

Ethical Issues

Professional integrity played a key role in my approach to the study. The British Sociological Association (BSA) suggests in their Statement of Ethical Practice that, "sociologists have a responsibility to ensure that the physical, social and psychological well-being of research participants is not adversely affected by the research" (BSA 2002:2). To ensure this was the case, participants were clearly informed about the research via a letter seeking the consent of participants (see Appendices 1-3). Within this letter, participants were informed of my identity as a researcher: that of a Masters student with Brunel University. Information relating to the nature of the research – the aims, how it was to be conducted and the likely benefits that could emerge from it – was given. Next, participants were told of the contributions they were expected to make and how much of their time it was likely to take. A consent form was attached, explaining that this did not commit anyone to the research and that participants could opt out at any time. The system for maintaining anonymity and confidentiality for participants and their organisations was fully explained, as well as the security arrangements for the collected data. The system entailed a code being given to each participant, whether they were involved in the focus groups, questionnaires or interviews. Their names were not be used at all. The names of their placements or first posts were not used within the transcriptions or any reference made to the identity of placements. Indeed, I did not record work places or names of co-workers but, where necessary, I would state the context of placements and first posts, as this information would inform the study. Transcriptions, questionnaires and tape recordings were all kept within a locked filing cabinet that was accessed by only me.

Researcher Role

Denscombe (2003) recognises the fact that the 'self' impacts in research analysis and that the researcher should be clear about their values and beliefs that could play a part in the production and analysis of qualitative data. What Denscombe is talking about here is reflexivity, which refers to the relationship between the researcher and the social world she is researching (Denscombe 2003:240). Denscombe further states that the researcher should explain how the research agenda has been shaped by personal experiences and social backgrounds. In my case, personal experience motivated me to undertake this research as I had been a student on the CYM course and experienced a very intense time of transition when I graduated. Also, I am a tutor on the course and have therefore gained insight from a different perspective. In this regard, I would suggest that I am in the best possible position to conduct this research, having had a first hand experience as a student, graduate and tutor. I see this as something to be celebrated and it has certainly added weight to the research. The idea of reflexivity is not necessarily negative, as Shelef (1994) suggests:

> Presupposition and bias of the researcher are both discovered and identified and then utilized to develop other questions to help in the investigation of the phenomenon...It is the interaction of the researcher wanting to know and the co-researcher (subjects) wanting to tell that can in itself create a simple paradigm for scientific knowing. (Shelef 1994: np)

There is no need for me to be apologetic about the interaction between myself, as researcher, and the data. This study benefits from the element of acknowledged personal position and informs the findings rather than invalidates them. Indeed, my familiarity with the field is a good starting point. I already had a rapport with the participants and understood the nuances of professional language and behaviour.

However, I do understand that there are potential drawbacks with this position. There could have been a potential for over-familiarity that may blind me to some important insights arising during the analysis stage. My role as tutor at CYM could have unduly biased the data, as participants may believe that I already hold a particular view on certain issues and therefore might have responded to the questions in a way that they thought I wanted to hear. There may have been power issues involved in that participants may have felt flattered at being chosen and wanted to be involved purely on that basis. This would then affect informed consent if there was participation out of a sense of 'flattery' and not because they felt they had positive input to offer (BSA, paragraphs 13 to 17). Also, if participants were to refuse, they may have been concerned that any future working relationship with CYM could be jeopardised. In practice, my awareness of these issues minimised the problems and helped me take them into account when analysing the data. These issues were reduced by recruiting those graduates who I had little or no professional contact with, through CYM or any other area of the field.

The phenomenological inquiry undertaken has provided me with a rich source of data, which I will be analysing in the following chapter. The case study approach offered a wide range of data from various perspectives and I view the case study approach as being the most appropriate qualitative strategy for this particular study.

Conclusion

I have discussed how a case study approach is the strongest methodology for the study of the relationship between the youth worker and their new professional world. As a researcher, I was entirely reliant on the participants and their willingness to co-operate within the research. I am grateful to them, not only for their co-operation but also for their interest in the topic itself. The next chapter will analyse the data collected from the participants, identifying key themes that will explain the professional socialisation for graduating youth workers.

Chapter Four

Data Analysis

This chapter provides analysis of the data collected. It contains a summary analysis of the thirteen questionnaires and ten semi-structured interviews. The focus groups material has not been analysed in the same way, as they were used to raise the issues that would enable me to conduct the study. However, the participants within the focus groups did raise some important points and these are included within the body of the findings.

Quotations within this chapter are taken from the focus groups, questionnaires and interview transcripts. These will be distinguished in the following way:

- F1 for focus group 1
- F2 for focus group 2

- the questionnaires carry the code S, followed by a number, S01 for questionnaire 1, S02 for questionnaire 2 and so on
- the interview transcripts will be marked with the codes A for the first participant, B for the second and so on.

The data has been reduced from masses of text by developing categories that provide a coherent and logical description of the findings. An open coding system was used that involved breaking down the data, comparing and examining it and then, finally, grouping it into categories. As the research project is essentially a phenomenological study, Moustakas (1994, quoted in Rudestam and Newton, 2001:157) suggests seven steps for the analysis of such a study:

1) Review each statement and how well it describes the experience

2) Record relevant statements

3) Remove redundant or overlapping statements, leaving the key meaning statements

4) Organise relevant meaning statements into themes

5) Merge themes into a description of the experience, use quotes from the text to supplement the description

6) Use the imagination and begin to find possible meanings in the text

7) Create a structure based on the text and provide meanings and the essence of the experience.

For the purposes of this chapter I have followed steps 1 to 5 as steps 6 and 7 adhere to the Data Discussion chapter following.

General Findings

Overall the findings suggest that participants felt prepared to enter the arena of work after completing the CYM course. The main issues arose from the professional socialisation period. The findings demonstrate a transitional phase for the participants, which will be discussed in closer detail in Chapter Five.

Impact of the Course

"The course taught us to think for ourselves and in a sense it trained up new leaders" (F1). This was the view of one of the members of the first focus group. The course was generally viewed as having created youth workers who were self aware and ready to take on a new challenge once graduated. *"I learnt things about myself on the course and I broadened my theoretical knowledge"* (D). Another participant commented about how the course changed his view of youth work being a career:

> I had done voluntary youth work before, I think the professional thing comes into it because when you do it voluntary, helping out a few hours a week or whatever, it doesn't seem like a career but when you come here you look at it that way (F2).

This change in perception of what it means to be a professional youth worker was very clear. *"The practical experience of working in my placement gave me a professionalism that I have been able to bring into my current job"* (G).

Participants spoke about their working lives before joining the course, whether positive or negative, and how these had been an influence on considering youth work as a profession. H mentioned his original reasons for starting the course and how these remained an influence in deciding on his first post:

> One of the reasons for joining the course was that I wanted to be able to work within the secular world, but trying to get the Christian message across, so that has always been my motivation for joining the course. (H)

Participant C discussed how she did not think church was right for her to work in due to a prior negative experience. Her ethos of working with young people was very different to that expected by churches and she therefore believed it impossible to 'fit in'. D stated that his decision not to work for a church was also related to previous negative experiences. These experiences of 'church', however, did not blur their sense of vocation or 'calling' to youth work. Some participants were absolutely certain that they were working in the right place: *"the salary is really low and accommodation is not provided...but I just had to decide what was important to me"* (J); *"I wanted to be in a place where I would be supporting young people who didn't know love at all, let alone God's love"* (C). Graduates had mostly positive experiences during their time on the course, however, and they had learnt what it meant to be a full-time professional youth worker. Nevertheless, the first post experience was traumatic for some.

Feelings

The responses of the participants to the question of what their feelings were when they started their first post mostly focused on emotions that were rooted in self-doubt. Comments included: *"I felt completely inadequate for the job, maybe not completely, but maybe 90% inadequate"* (B) and *"it's a bit scary"* (A). Many of the participants spoke of feeling anxious about decision-making and overwhelmed at the amount of responsibility now facing them. A talks about his first few weeks in a new post and reflects on how he felt:

> *There's a lot to take in and well there's stuff that people have been used to for ages and you don't know who's who or what's what and so you feel you have to learn so much...it was like you're the youth worker now so here's the office and there you*

go but I didn't know what to do for a good two or three weeks'.
(A)

Most participants spoke of feeling nervous and unsure: *"I was very unsure of myself"* (S10). F also comments, *"the words that would come out of my mouth seemed to be the wrong ones,"* but he put this down to being nervous. One participant who had been in post just a matter of weeks when interviewed said that he did not have enough self-belief. Another remarked, *"I thought I was going to fall flat on my face"* (D). H commented that, *"The worst thing when I left CYM and started my job was that the buck stopped with me, it was really scary"* (H).

However, others were incredibly excited by the new opportunities ahead of them: *"I was incredibly excited, just like being given a new lease of life"* (E); *"I felt really chuffed to have been chosen for such a great job, it really boosted my confidence"* (K).

Expectations

Some participants experienced feelings and issues that they did not expect to have. One participant, A, remarked on how he gave a professional persona at the interview but, now that he had started the post, the organisation itself was not very professional.

Almost all the participants experienced extremes of emotion when they first started their posts and talked of feeling enthusiastic, scared, relieved, bewildered, energised, exhausted, confident and unconfident (S02, S03, S06, S07, S012, S13, S08, A, D, E, F, H, J, K). These extremes of emotion and feelings related to a number of issues; not all of them related to the actual work. Moving to a completely new area and personal circumstances, such as being a spouse and parent, were cited as issues. J spoke about how coming to a new place really enthused her initially but this was followed with feeling completely overwhelmed and lonely:

> *I was quite surprised at...the loneliness, I wasn't expecting to feel like that because I don't generally have problems making friends but I think it was because I moved somewhere which was completely new.* (J)

S12 comments, *"starting a full-time post was a real shock in terms of my time and trying to juggle family life too."* Another participant experienced a similar issue: *"getting used to working full-time was a big issue, not having done that for many years, and having to re-juggle life as a mum and wife"* (S07).

Participant S04 spoke of the difficulty with the low expectations that his employers held. As a result of this, he had to challenge their view of what a youth worker was and the purpose of effective youth work. One participant partly blamed her management team for her decision to leave her post: *"when our values differed it caused massive problems, they wanted to change the direction of the work and it was all very badly managed"* (S06).

Impressions

Perhaps expectations had been too high for some participants but making a good impression was an important goal for others. Some wanted to appear professional to their employers, even if they did not necessarily feel professional. As a result, some felt they were being fake and felt uncomfortable with the amount of trust that was being placed in them and in their abilities when they did not necessarily feel worthy of such trust: *"I was scared at the amount of trust being put in me, because at college you were challenged a lot about everything and now that didn't happen"* (S11).

Mixing with other professionals brought on feelings of intimidation and an awareness of age, especially for the younger graduates, who were almost apologetic for being in their early twenties and involved in partnership work at a strategic level:

> *The biggest problem I had when I started was that I was just very young and I noticed it and others did too and in the position I was in I was sitting in rooms with people who had loads more experience than me and I was at the same level as them and you could see them going, well, what?* (C)

Again,

> *I was nervous and worried, one of the things that really made me nervous were you know, the volunteers who were mature adults and I was like here I am 24 years old and fresh out of college and I was worried about oh are they going to respect me?* (G)

For those who did feel intimidated, there was an added pressure; that of wanting to be taken seriously: *"I knew that I knew my stuff and I wanted to be taken seriously"* (C); *"I would sit at meetings surrounded by really experienced professionals and I just wanted to let them know that I had spent years working with young people and they should listen to what I had to say"* (K). Another participant from Focus Group 1, reflecting on their first post, commented that, *"I did a lot more than I ever thought I would do and got lots of respect for it"* (F1). This does not necessarily have to be a negative time but very much depends on the youth worker themselves and their attitude to the work and also on the support they have during this time.

Performance

The desire to perform well was a driving force for some participants. H, for example, discussed how he experienced this:

> *I wanted to perform, but you can't perform until you work out what's going on and what needs to happen. So there is a pressure of wanting to perform and holding on to what is right and make those good decisions.* (H)

Many participants started working for organisations that were completely different to the fieldwork placements they had been involved with for the three years of the course. These differences were predominantly to do with structure, culture, ethos and values. Six out of the ten interviewees had moved from a Christian placement to a secular post, or secular type work within a Christian setting. Issues ranged from having to complete more paper work to becoming directly involved with Children's Trusts and other government initiatives. What became apparent was that those graduates who did not have any significant work experience outside the Christian sector struggled the most with these issues, including: *"I did not understand strategic thinking, specific departments within a local authority or government policies"* (S08); *"funding bids were new to me and the language we had to use, also, government initiatives were not well known to me"* (S03). Information overload was another hurdle to jump for some participants: *"I had a lot of ground work to cover myself"* (S12); *"I had loads of policies and reading to do about the organisation, which took up loads of my time"* (S03). Other issues included, *"Understanding the workings of and how to work with local authority youth agencies"* (S04). Partnership working featured as a concern for other participants too:

> *I was suddenly sitting around a table with loads of other people from other agencies and I didn't really have a clue who any of*

them were....so I would sit really quietly until I was really sure of what I needed to say, I just wasn't sure how to be. (K)

Management responsibilities in the new post unsettled some participants. Participant H commented, *"I think youth work is one of the few fields where you are given a lot of responsibility without the experience of management"* (H). B noted that, *"Writing business plans and that is all new to me. I wish I had had more experience in that sort of thing before I had started the job"* (B). A further comment was, *"My time was really taken up with management issues and at times I could not manage it all effectively"* (S03). However hard this performance phase was for the participants, their determination and commitment to young people was paramount and, for some, they sensed that they would not feel like this forever.

Integration

There were issues regarding change for those graduates who stayed within Church youth work, but changed denomination: *"my biggest problem was understanding the workings of the URC (United Reformed Church)"* (S04); *"I needed to have a real understanding of confirmation and baptism because I was going to be running those classes for some young people, but I didn't have a clue"* (G). Change of organisation appears to have had a significant impact on the participants. This was also accompanied with a change in the culture of young people they were now working with:

Here there are probably one or two young people who would be regarded as 'stable', I mainly work with young people who are tagged, have serious criminal records, use drugs nearly every day, can't read or write and live in a level of poverty that I never expected to see in Britain. (J)

Other participants spoke of having to 'deconstruct' when they left the course and started their first posts:

> *I recognised, which surprised me, that I needed to almost deconstruct a little bit again...I realised that it can be quite dangerous going into a new environment and saying 'yea, I've been there and done that' when actually you haven't...I needed to explore my values again, what I learnt before and how does that fit now?* (F)

B also commented, *"I had to peel back all my learning from the course when I started my job and really look at what was important in youth work that could be applied to my new place."* One graduate who reflected on his transition from the Christian voluntary sector remarked:

> *A lot of my learning had been done within the context of church based youth work and when I got my post with the local authority, my thinking was, the principles of youth work are the same, but the application looks quite different in this environment.* (F)

Another participant remarked how it was not the environment that affected this deconstruction phase so much as her own self: *"The expectations of myself changed rather than other stuff around me"* (F1). Looking back to the past to inform the present is a positive aspect in the professional development of the youth worker. Again, depending on the youth worker and their environment, this could be a disturbing experience. However, the important aspect to draw from this phase is the clear development of professional identity.

Professional Identity

The study revealed a strong sense of professional identity in some of the participants. When asked if her practice with young people had changed in the past two years, K said, *"Hugely, I am a professional youth worker now and I didn't really know what that meant"* (K). This reflects a definite change in the professional identity of this participant from when they graduated from the course. Recognising the relationship between self and professional identity, K continued, *"I feel I have grown up as a person and as a professional."*

Some graduates expressed concern about a lower standard of professionalism with their managers in their new posts. However, some saw this as a positive attribute that they would bring to the post. This was certainly the case for some participants who entered church posts:

> *I've been handled unprofessionally because they just don't know what to do and they've never had this before, but I think this is something I can bring to the post because when I did the interview they said they were impressed that I had training and came across as professional* (A).

The nature of professionalism is worth raising here. Participants used the word 'professional' many times throughout the study. In the first Focus Group, the participants continually referred to 'being professional'. I asked them for clarity on what they meant by 'professional' but they had great difficulty in defining it. One person said, *"its about knowing how to do risk assessments, what forms to fill in, making sure the health and safety policy is being done"* (F1). Another commented, *"I think in one sense it's abiding by the rules and regulations of the work place"* (F1). Eventually the group began to discuss it on a deeper level:

> *I think it's about knowing yourself really well, lots of things around you might change, like policy, people you work with and stuff like that, but if you are self-aware and can hold onto the principles of youth work in it all, then you will do ok.* (F1)

An interesting theme that emerged was that of the need for graduates to reassess their idea of professional youth work once they started their first posts:

> *It's funny actually because I came here with different boundaries to what I've got now I would really have been a lot more strict about things before but now, just because of the mood of the young people I've changed a lot in the way I do things.* (J)

Another participant spoke of similar issues: *"What I learnt at CYM has enabled me to find the position I'm in now but it took another three years to distil it all (knowledge) and come out with something"* (D). Professional identity formation is evident in every process of the professional socialisation period. These issues are particularly dominant in how services are delivered today, with partnership working high on the government agenda. In order to develop a healthy professional identity, support structures play a vital role.

Support Structures

There was not one participant in the whole of the study who did not find support from another person as a valuable aspect within their work. When asked if they had any support structures in place in their first post, the participants recalled a number of various people in various roles – apart from line managers, students mentioned mentors, pastoral support, spiritual directors and non-managerial support. Therefore, support is viewed as being those individuals who fulfil a specific role that will aid the youth worker in a number of ways, be that in direction for the work, reflecting on practice, spiritual development and/or help with personal issues. What is striking about this is that nearly all the participants either maintained an aspect of support that had been developed while they were at college, or sought to find new support due to a long distance move. Participants S07 and G, for example, both had support from their line managers but, feeling it was not enough, found non-managerial support. Participant D spoke of someone in his first post who, *"kind of took me under his wing and he was really respected by everyone"* (D). Also, *"As I worked in a secular agency I found my own spiritual support"* (S10). K commented, *"I made contact with my old fieldwork tutor and asked if she would be happy to meet with me every so often to help me reflect on my practice"* (K). It appears that this high level of importance placed on support structures originates from the importance that the CYM course places on support.

Participants were asked what they missed most about the course when they left. Most of the answers focused on support systems. The responses consisted of a mix of missing the informal as well as formal structures:

> *I mostly missed the family – fellow students, staff, co-workers and young people – both in terms of the friendships and relationships there and of the challenge, which they brought on a youth work level.* (S01)

Different modes of support, it seems, is a key factor in enabling a smooth transition into the new working environment for CYM students. Other elements of the course that were missed by some participants were, *"being able to discuss my practice in a supportive and challenging environment"* (S03), *"the reflective time together"* (G) and *"being able to reflect and having time to look at theories"* (C). Reflective practice and having a forum to articulate this had a positive impact on the participants while they were students but then was desperately missed once they graduated.

Conclusion

The key points drawn from the data collected exhibit a transitional phase. These range from

1) The impact of the course on the learning and development of the participants

2) Feelings that participants experienced when the began their first post

3) Expectations that participants had about being a full-time worker

4) Impressions that participants wanted to make on employers and other professionals

5) The performance that participants conducted in ensuring they were seen as professional

6) The integration of learning within the first post

7) Issues relating to professional identity and

8) The importance of support structures for the professional socialisation of youth workers.

These findings will now be interpreted in light of the existing literature and theories reviewed in Chapter Two.

Chapter Five

Interpretation and Discussion

This chapter will discuss the significant findings from the research undertaken with participants who have gradated from the CYM course in Cambridge. First, I will provide an overview of the findings. Second, I will consider the findings in light of the literature analysed in the literature review.

Overview of the Findings

The findings focused around the eight key themes outlined in the Conclusion to the last chapter. To recap, the key points that emerged from the literature review were:

1) The transitional stages of professional socialisation

2) The transitional stages of career socialisation

3) The concept of micro-socialisation

4) Informal and formal mechanisms of professional socialisation

5) The impact of organisational socialisation and

6) Professional Identity as a product of the professional socialisation process. The findings from my research provided clear evidence that the participants embarked on a transitional phase once they had graduated from CYM and started their first full-time posts. This mirrors the stages of professional socialisation offered by Davis (1968). Although it is true to say that, when the stages are applied to new professionals, it is not a mechanistic process, they do provide a broad understanding of their experiences. The stages, corresponding with the findings above, will provide a framework for interpretation and discussion of my own work in this chapter and will be used alongside additional ideas drawn from other literature to theorise the data.

Initial Innocence

Initial innocence is the first stage of transition experienced by the newly qualified professional youth worker. Davis viewed this as the stage where feelings of worry and disappointment are dominant. Graduates have left behind the safety of the course to embark on a new phase of their lives after three years of preparation. The findings of this study show that the feelings of participants, when they began their first posts, mirrored those described by Davis (1968). This is a time "filled with feelings of embarrassment, uselessness, and personal inadequacy" (1968:242). These feelings of inadequacy, anxiety and worry abounded for participants (see Chapter Four). These anxious feelings are not specific to graduating youth workers. Indeed, it is a common feeling to be nervous upon embarking on any new post. It has been commented that, "the transition to working life can be said to be a difficult one in all professions" (Kremer-Hayon & Ben-Peretz 1986:413). However, for the graduating youth worker this stage appears to be particularly worrying as youth work brings with it a specific set of concerns. Youth work has been subject to dramatic changes over the past few years. With the introduction of *Every Child Matters* and Children's Trusts, youth workers have to respond to fundamental changes in how services are delivered. Preparation for graduates can be difficult, as the delivery of these services looks different in each locality. These wider factors, usually coupled with a change of organisation and perhaps location, make for an unsettling time, which also impacts on the professional identity of the youth worker.

The relationship between professional socialisation and professional identity are closely related. These findings show that youth workers leave their course absolutely certain that they are 'youth workers'. This being the case, Davis (1968) would say that youth workers had already attained the sixth stage, that of stable internalization. However, I suggest that the issues described above cause the graduates to reassess their position in terms of who they are in relation to what is going on around them. As Erikson (1950) wrote, "identity is never gained nor maintained once and for all" (1950:57). The new professional identity of the youth worker will be constantly developing through the insights they are gaining from full-time professional practice. Conclusion at end

Youth workers on the CYM course have a work placement for the duration and are therefore already aware of issues within the field, such as, *Every Child Matters* and Children's Trusts. This study reveals that it is the sense of loss experienced by graduates, moving to a new organisation, overload of information and having to learn about policies that will have a bearing on their work, that brought on the range of feelings and emotions described in Chapter Four. The socialisation of the youth worker at this stage is largely dependent on the organisation that employs the youth worker. If the organisation is supportive to the new graduate, the shift during this stage can be full of excitement and promise for the youth worker. However, if the organisation has poor management structures, or too high or too low expectations of the youth worker, difficulties occur. These may include lack of accountability, lack of direction for the work or management responsibilities beyond their capacity. The professional knowledge already attained by the youth worker, the professional identity of the youth worker and the professionalism of the organisation all have bearing on initial innocence and how it is managed. The successful transition through this phase leads onto what Davis describes as 'labelled recognition of incongruity'.

Labelled Recognition of Incongruity

Davis describes this stage as a time of soul-searching due to the realisation that the profession is not all they thought it would be (Davis, 1968). The findings from my research show that the new youth workers' expectations about their new post were not congruent with what they had imagined (Chapter Four). It is true to say that youth workers do not come into the profession for the financial rewards. Rates of pay were never discussed, apart from one youth worker who was receiving an appallingly low amount. Even so, this did not sway her commitment to the post. Corcoran and Clark's study (1984), and their three-stage model of career socialisation, has something to offer in explaining this phase. The third stage, role continuance, is applicable here as it takes into account the difficulties that individuals may face during this time. This is not to be confused with the work of Davis but Corcoran and Clark's role continuance provides further understanding of issues that can occur within a full-time post. Corcoran and Clark comment that, if reward and opportunities are lacking and there is less on offer than what was expected (1984:135), the individual is likely to experience doubts about their chosen profession. My findings have shown that some participants did experience this sense of doubt and that the consequences were detrimental to the profession. Indeed, as indicated in Chapter Four, one of the youth workers who completed a questionnaire left the profession within a few months of starting her first post, due to expectations not being fulfilled.

The implications of this stage on the field of youth work and training are enormous. Newly qualified youth workers graduate with a high level of knowledge and expertise that has been developed within a supportive training environment for three years. The expectations on the graduate can be too high. Using the example of newly qualified teachers, they usually begin work within an environment that consists of other professional teachers. They can discuss, learn and be supported by this environment, as discussed by Moon *et al* (2000), referred to in Chapter Two. As the data has shown, the newly qualified youth worker, especially within a church setting, can be isolated, managing a large team of volunteers, charged with development of the work with little time for reflection on their practice. The zeal with which graduates left the course can soon be crushed. The harsh realities of the post can push a new youth worker to leave the profession altogether. This highlights a challenge to churches and other organisations; be they charities or, indeed, local authorities. An understanding of what a newly qualified youth worker is prepared for must be developed. The findings from this study state that there is sometimes a mismatch between the knowledge and skills of a newly qualified youth worker and that of the high expectations of an organisation of the new youth worker. This usually pertains to management issues and the amount of responsibility placed on new graduates.

If youth workers manage to move through this phase then they may move on to the stage defined by Davis as 'psyching out'.

Psyching Out

By 'psyching out', Davis refers to the stage when individuals work out what is expected of them from those in authority over them. This phase can occur when youth workers work out what is required of them within their particular context. Potentially, this leads to feelings of personal inauthenticity. This appears to be an important developmental stage for the ongoing professional identity of the youth worker. Payne (2004) views managerial responsibilities as being particularly influential for professional identity. This is an area for investigation concerning the professional identity of the youth worker. As already mentioned, Children's Trusts are becoming established across the country, the focus on partnership work is on the increase and youth workers are experiencing a shift in their practice towards work within multi-disciplinary teams. The effect of this on the youth worker, who may be undergoing a 'psyching out' phase, could be enormous. The impact of this may not only be on the youth worker but on those who are working in partnership with the youth worker. Wenger (1998) views identity as a "nexus of multi membership" (1998:163) and goes on to comment that, "...we define who we are by the ways we experience our selves through participation as well as by the ways we and others reify ourselves" (1998:149). If an understanding of the professional identity of a youth worker were ever straightforward, this suggests that identity for a youth worker has become much more complex and changing than ever before. The research of Opie (2003), cited in Payne (2004), on multi-professional teamwork, found that the negotiation of role within a multi-disciplinary team was not about traditional understandings so much as the use of different kinds of knowledge and understanding in that particular setting (2004:5).

For the newly qualified youth worker, then, this early point in their career could be their first experience of partnership work. The participants in this study had not had many opportunities to work in partnership before graduating from the course. The course provides teaching on partnership but the actual experiences of such work are limited. The leap from student to full-time worker, in relation to partnership work, raises significant issues for the youth worker and the field, especially in terms of professional identity. This will be discussed further in the next stage of 'role simulation'.

Role Simulation

This is the performance of psyching out. By this, Davis means that the individual acts out the role that he or she thinks is expected by those in authority over them. The uncomfortable feeling of being 'fake' that accompanies this stage was discussed by many of the participants (Chapter Four). The study revealed that there was a need for participants to feel like they were being genuine in their work with young people. The data raised key issues around participants being aware of themselves and the need for creating a good impression on colleagues and especially those they worked with in partnership. The stage of role simulation involves the acting out of the identity issues just discussed in the psyching out phase. For the profession, this could either be a time for youth workers to shine or it could be a time for them to be seen as unnecessary or ill equipped to work alongside other organisations in a professional manner. The success of this phase will rest on the youth worker's ability to make sense of what is happening to them and the sense of professional identity they had already brought with them. The training of the youth worker, in terms of their knowledge and skills, needs to be of a high standard in order for them to be able to develop their professional identity with as little stress involved as possible. The identities formed by new youth workers during this phase could influence how the profession is seen more widely. Again, this could be positive or negative depending on the particular youth worker and the success of this phase.

Provisional Internalization

This is the stage that Davis refers to as the experience of recurrent vacillation between commitment to the new professional identity and attachment to the old. Wenger (1998) sees identity as a course of learning that, "incorporates the past and the future in the very process of negotiating the present" (1998:74). Some participants in this study spoke of their past and the impact that had on their decision to go into youth work and then on their decision about taking their first post. The findings suggested that experiences from the past had bearing on their current role. The terminology used by some participants must be noted

– that of 'calling' or 'vocation' – which implies a higher level of commitment and aspiration. Indeed, a strong sense of identity arising from a sense of calling was evident within the findings. The youth worker's identity has already been developing before entering the course. This is due to the requirement of the course that potential students must have at least 300 hours experience prior to joining the course (CYM Prospectus: 2007). Most participants had undergone a voluntary experience of youth work before starting the course. Youth workers exiting from the CYM course therefore have an advantage when it comes to professional socialisation, as they have had a good period of pre-course preparation. Youth work can be seen as having a valuable contribution to make to the study of professional socialisation, especially in the area of prior experience and volunteering.

Stable Internalization

Davis (1968) describes stable internalization as the time when the individuals firmly believe themselves to be professionals, "of a particular doctrinal persuasion" (1968:250). On the basis of the findings in this study, it is apparent that the youth worker, once established within their post with the transitional issues behind them, now has a developed sense of professional identity. However, this strong sense of identity is only apparent in those graduates who have undergone a successful journey through the stages. This successful journey is marked by a prepared and understanding organisation, a well-supported and strong management structure, a strong sense of professional identity of the youth worker and an ongoing commitment to the profession.

In their research into the socialisation of English teachers, Marshal *et al* identified how some of the participants in the study had "slightly relaxed" (2001:194) their beliefs on issues they had once held to firmly. The reason for this was due to the particular school that the teachers were working in. They found that the teachers still held onto the underlying principles developed during their training but the actual teaching as a qualified professional meant that some realised the need to shift their viewpoints in order to meet the demands of their posts. Thus, their professional identity continued to be in an ongoing process, in relation to the issues at work around them. This highlights the tension between the aspirations of teachers and the constraints that are placed on them in terms of policy and the working environment. Youth workers face similar challenges. Indeed, interviewees identified policy constraints and working environment as having an impact on the their professional identity, be that Christian or secular. Reconstructions occur within this stage and my research showed that many youth workers had either come through this stage or were experiencing it during the research.

Stable internalization does not suggest that the development of professional identity ceases (Davis 1968:250). The work of Payne (2004) suggests that contemporary perspectives on identity view it as a lifelong process (Payne: 2004). In fact, Payne develops this further by taking into account external factors such as managerial responsibilities and working in partnership as having an impact of identity formation. Perhaps not unexpectedly, some participants within the study had not achieved this phase due to the fact that they are all at different points in their careers; some had only been in post for a matter of weeks when they were interviewed. However, one main finding that the research identified was the importance of support for youth workers, whatever stage they were at, and thereby enabling them to engage in ongoing 'identity work'.

Support Structures

Davis does not allude to the notion of support within his work. However, all the participants made some reference to the importance of having 'someone' with whom to talk. Therefore, it is a key area for discussion and one that can be applied to all stages of professional socialisation. The support that is being discussed refers to those individuals who are assigned or adopt specific roles that aid the youth worker in some capacity. This could be a 'good' line manager, a supervisor in a non-managerial capacity (if required), a mentor who will help the youth worker to reflect on their practice and development and/or a pastoral support person who may listen to more personal issues that the youth worker may have.

The data provides a clear indication that support is considered important throughout all the stages of professional socialisation. Kremer-Hayon and Ben-Peretz (1986) found conflicting opinions amongst teachers when it came to their support structures and accountability. Some teachers appreciated close support whilst others felt that they did not acquire the independence they were seeking because of it. On the CYM course, accountability structures are considered vital for the professional youth worker. These structures are set in the areas of supervision that the student is exposed to on the course (see Chapter One) and are there for the reasons discussed; that of professional formation, reflection on practice or personal issues. As all participants in this study saw the importance of such support structures, and where they were lacking within their posts, the participants proactively sought them out. Support for youth workers when they are first employed and, throughout their careers, is a crucial aspect of their ongoing professional development. This was overwhelmingly apparent with the findings of this study. However, the organisations that youth workers find themselves working in offer varying levels of support. Again, there is a challenge being issued towards these organisations for which support is not viewed as essential for a new employee. There should be an understanding of what the requirements are in terms of accountability. Therefore, the employer could provide strong line management or non-managerial support as well as pastoral or mentoring.

This chapter has interpreted the findings in light of Davis' six stages and other relevant literature. The following chapter will draw the main conclusions from the research undertaken for this dissertation.

Chapter Six

Conclusion

This dissertation is concerned with the professional socialisation of graduating youth workers as they embark on their first full-time post. It is a phenomenological study exploring the sociological issues that impact on graduating youth workers as they make the transition into professional full-time youth work. The data has provided a broad understanding of professional socialisation issues for professional youth workers. The work of Davis (1968), explored in Chapter Two, has provided an understanding of the transitional phases of professional socialisation. The six stages he outlined have been used as a framework in developing an understanding of the issues faced by newly qualified youth workers.

Implications for the field

The data analysis suggests that management issues in a first post may have detrimental effects on the socialisation process. These issues included a lack of adequate management in the new post, high expectations of what a newly qualified youth worker was capable of or, in some cases, low expectations. Youth work is one of the few professional fields that expect a high level of management from a newly qualified worker. New full-time youth workers are expected to line manage a number of part time or volunteer youth workers. Other responsibilities include; management of projects, development of the work, writing of funding applications, working in partnership with other agencies, managing buildings, as well as ensuring that health and safety and child protection policies are maintained and implemented. These are huge responsibilities for a newly qualified worker. Becker *et al* (1961), in 'Boys in White', discussed how professional training is now part of the experience of a large number of young people in society. Although this was first written in 1961, it is true for today, especially for youth work training, which seems to attract younger people; those under the age of twenty-five. The majority of students on the CYM course at the present time may be fully adult, physically and socially – indeed, some are married with children – but most fall into the category of being young people themselves. However, as Becker *et al* suggested, once graduated they still have a long period ahead of them, in terms of gaining experience in the 'real world' of professional youth work. They need to experience what Becker *et al* describes as "a sort of adolescence" (1961:5), during which time they are to show adult competence and learning, without being given the full adult responsibility. This is a huge challenge to the field of professional youth work. However, if the new professionals joining the field are to become competent, highly skilled youth workers who can create a strong professional identity, the professional youth worker role needs to be reassessed.

This study reveals that support structures for newly qualified youth workers are vital, not only in the early stages of their professional formation, but throughout the early stages of their careers. Youth workers find that being managed well, having pastoral support or a mentor and friends within the field is invaluable in aiding their continual professional development. Apart from line management, these roles (non-managerial support, pastoral support and mentors) are not mandatory. This important aspect during the socialisation period is therefore often neglected. A reason why these non-mandatory relationships are successful is that the youth worker is able to *choose* these people to fulfil these roles. I view this as an important aspect to be maintained. The employers of youth workers need to consider these roles when they are creating posts. Providing time and expenses for youth workers to pursue these relationships would enable youth workers to continue their development. They would also feel valued by the organisation, increasing effective socialisation.

Implications for CYM

Generally, the study finds CYM students to be prepared for their first full-time post on graduating from the course. The strengths of CYM graduates are in their commitment to young people and the profession, even under difficult circumstances. CYM graduates are also able to 'professionalize' new places of employment, where the professional element is found to be lacking. The weaker areas of CYM graduates are found in awareness of professional identity issues; for example, who they are as youth workers in relation to other professionals. There is considerable focus on developing the youth worker during the period of study. However, there is little input given into the processes and issues that will affect the youth worker once they have graduated. A reason for this may be because of the lack of research conducted in this area, until now. I recommend that CYM introduce specific teaching on professional socialisation and professional identity into the course. This study reveals that it is upon leaving the course and beginning their first posts that graduates realised the importance of such knowledge. The stages of transition proposed by Davis, and used here, alongside the theories of career and organisational socialisation, have much to offer students about to graduate. The third year is a time when youth workers are deciding what type of youth work they want to do; Christian or secular. Teaching on these issues could help youth workers develop a deeper understanding of their professional identity in whatever field they consequently pursue.

Implications for graduating youth workers

The study finds that the professional socialisation process for graduating youth workers is a time that is affected by many external factors. The impact of government initiatives, such as Children's Trusts and the focus on partnership work, organisational and career socialisation all impact on the professional identity of the youth worker. The work of Niemi (1997) (cited in Adams *et al* 2006) discusses how the process by which professional identity forms and develops does not process in a linear way. This study did not explore the impact of professional identity on practice, and ultimately on young people, and this could be an area for future research. There is a responsibility placed on the graduate in that professional development is a proactive endeavour. Looking for learning opportunities that will continue to enhance and develop their knowledge and practice will aid the youth worker in their development. Being aware of the issues during socialisation (self-doubt, worry, needing to impress, information overload, organisational changes and so on) will enable youth workers to make quicker and less troubling times of change, as well as ensuring that youth workers will want to remain within the field.

Limitation of the Research

In reflecting on my research I am conscious of its limitations. The first limitation to note is due to the sample of participants used for the study. The sample involved participants who had just graduated from the course; just a matter of three months, to those who had graduated from the course some six years previously. I found those who had graduated the longest from the course to have a more nostalgic outlook on their first post. Those who were fresh into their posts did provide the richest data in terms of being able to speak directly and 'in the moment' about their experiences. If I could conduct the research again, I would interview participants who had graduated no more than two years from the course, as the professional socialisation process would still be fresh.

Another limitation is that of making generalisations from the case study. Participants all came from the Cambridge Centre. Although some generalisations can be made about professional socialisation from this, especially in terms of the issues involved, it may not be possible to generalise about every finding. The fact that most participants worked either in London or Cambridge may have an impact on the findings since these two cities offer very different cultural settings. Focusing on youth workers within one particular town or city may have offer further research a more clearly defined picture of the major issues.

Finally, researching youth workers who worked within the Christian and secular environments brings its problems. There was a range of personal beliefs and values that made the boundaries of the research difficult to manage. Research aimed specifically at one group or the other would provide clearer findings in regard to this aspect.

Further Research

The study has raised a number of questions that would be worth exploring. First, it has shown that youth workers exhibit a level of professional identity before entering a course. The voluntary sector of youth work, especially within the church and Christian organisations is the largest in Britain (Brierley, 2000). Therefore, the processes by which these have been formed before entering a course has much to offer to voluntary organisations and volunteers themselves. A fascinating arena for future research would be that of professional identity formation amongst volunteer youth workers.

Second, this research found that working in partnership with other agencies had an impact on the development of the professional identity of youth workers. Research is therefore needed to explore the effects of working within multi-disciplinary teams on the professional identity of youth workers. This is a key area for youth work research as the implementation of multi-disciplinary teams in the delivery of youth services to children and young people will have a massive impact on the future professional identity of youth workers. A longitudinal study, over a period of three years for example, would provide an in-depth and much needed investigation into the changes and development of professional identity.

The questions posed at the beginning of this project have received clear answers. The successful professional socialisation of the newly qualified youth worker into the profession is greatly dependent on a positive, healthy and well-supported first post. The education of student youth workers and training institutions around the issues that could hinder the process is vital in the creation of a professional, highly skilled and committed work force. The work discussed in this dissertation is intended to contribute to developing that education.

BIBLIOGRAPHY

Abercrombie, N., Hill, S. & Turner, B.S. (1984) Dictionary of
    Sociology, New York: Penguin Books

Adams, K., Hean, S., Sturgis, P. & Macleod Clark, J. 'Investigating the
    Factors Influencing Professional Identity of First-Year Health
    and Social Care Students', *Learning in Health and Social Care,*
    (2: 2006), 55–68. Blackwell Publishing Ltd

Becker, H.S., Geer, B., Hughes, E.C. & Strauss, A. (1961) Boys in
    White, Transaction Publishers: Chicago

Becker, H.S., Geer, B., Riesman, D., & Weiss, R.S. (eds) (1968)
    Institutions and the Person: Papers Presented to Everett C.
    Hughes, Chicago: Aldine Becker, H.S. & Strauss, A.I.,
    'Careers, Personality and Adult Socialisation', *The American
    Journal of Sociology,* (Nov: 1956), 253 – 263. The University
    of Chicago.

Bell, J. (2005) <u>Doing Your Research Project</u>, Maidenhead: Open
    University Press.

Brierley, P. (2000) <u>The Tide is Running Out</u>, London: Christian
    Research

British Sociological Association (2002) <u>Statement of Ethical Practice,</u>

Brunner, J. (1990) <u>Acts of Meaning,</u> Cambridge, MA: Harvard
    University Press

Bryman, A. (2004) <u>Social Research Methods</u> Oxford: Oxford
    University Press

Caires, S. & Almeida, L.S. 'Teaching practice in Initial Teacher
    Education: its impact on student teachers' professional skills and
    development', *Journal of Education for Teaching*, (2:2005), 111
    – 120. Taylor and Francis Group Ltd.

Carpenter, M.C. & Platt, S. 'Professional Identity for Clinical Social
    Workers: Impact of Changes in Health Care Delivery Systems',
    Clinical Social Work Journal, (3:1997), 337–350). Human
    Sciences Press, Inc.

Cole, P.M. (Spring 1994) *Finding A Path Through The Research Maze,*
    <u>The Qualitative Report</u>, Volume 2, Number 1,

Corcoran, M. & Clark, S.M. 'Professional Socialization and
    Contemporary Career Attitudes of Three Faculty Generations',
    Research in Higher Education, (2:1984), 131-153. Agathon
    Press, Inc.

CYM Prospectus (2007) *BA Hons Youth and Community Work with
    Applied Theology Degree* np

Denscombe, M. (2000) <u>The Good Research Guide</u>, Maidenhead: Open
    University Press

Dewey, J. (1997) <u>How We Think</u>, London: Dover Publications

Erikson, E. (1950) Childhood and Society, New York: W.W. Norton

Fidler, B. & Atton, T. (2003) The Headship Game: The Challenges of Contemporary School Leadership, New York:RoutledgeFalmer

Gillespie, R. & Moon, G. (eds), (1995) Society and Health: An Introduction to Social Science for Health Professionals, London: Routledge

Heath, A.W. (March 1997) *The Proposal in Qualitative Research*, *The Qualitative Report,* Volume 3, Number 1,

Jones, M. 'Fitting in, Feeling Excluded or Opting Out? An Investigation into the Socialisation Process of Newcomers to the Teaching Profession in Secondary Schools in England', *Journal of In-service Education*, (3:2005), 509–526. Routledge

Kremer-Hayon, L. & Ben-Peretz, M. 'Becoming a Teacher: The Transition from Teachers' College to Classroom Life', *International Review of Education xxxii,* (1986) 413–422, Hamburg and Martinus Nijhoff Publishers: Dordrecht.

Marshal, B., Turvey, A. & Brindley, 'English Teachers – Born or Made: a longitudinal study on the socialisation of English teachers', *Changing English* (2:2001), 189 – 201, Routledge: London.

Moon, B., Ben-Peretz, M. & Brown, S. (eds) (2000) Routledge International Companion to Education, Routledge: London

Moustakas, C. (1990) Heuristic Research: Design, Methodology, and Applications, Newbury Park, CA: Sage

Nicholson, P. (1996) Gender, Power & Organisation: A Psychological Perspective, Routledge: London

National Youth Agency (2007), www.nya.org.uk

Payne, M. 'Identities: An Agency Study of a Hospice' *British*

Association of Social Workers (1: 2004), 5–11.

Prince, K.J.A.H., Van de Wiel, M.W.J., Scherpbier, A.J.J.A., Van der Vleuten, C.P.M., Boshuizen, H.P.A., 'A Qualitative Analysis of the Transition from Theory to Practice in Undergraduate Training in a PBL – Medical School' *Advances in Health Sciences Education* (5:2000), 105–116. Kluwer Academic Publishers.

Richards, S. (2005) An Exploration of the Notion of 'Sense of Vocation' Among Christian Youthworkers, EdD Thesis: Kings College London, Unpublished.

Robson, J. 'Exploring the Professional Socialisation of Teachers in Further Education: a case study', *Teacher Development, Vol. 2, No. 1, 1998*

Roslender, R. (1992) Sociological Perspectives on Modern Accountancy, New York: Routledge

Rudestam, K. E. & Newton, R. R. (2001) Surviving Your Dissertation, London: Sage Publications Ltd.

Shelef, L.O, (Spring 1994), *A Simple Qualitative Paradigm: The Asking and The Telling,* The Qualitative Report, Volume 2, Number 1,

Wegner, E. (1998) Communities of Practice: Learning, Meaning and Identity, Cambridge: Cambridge University Press

APPENDIX ONE

Letter of Informed Consent:

Focus Groups

School of Sport and Education

Brunel University

Home address: 4 Broad Green Steeple Bumpstead, Suffolk CB9 7BW

Tel: 07732041998

Email:jfg33@cam.ac.uk

Thank you for agreeing to participate in this research.

This research is being conducted for a dissertation as part of an MA in Youth & Community studies at Brunel University. The dissertation topic is the professional socialisation of graduating youth workers into full time employment. I will be conducting a case study with participants who graduated from CYM Cambridge. The aim of the study is to find out what the professional socialisation issues are for graduating youth workers and how CYM can better prepare students for these issues.

The data will be collected using 2 focus groups, questionnaires and semi-structured interviews. You are invited to take part in a focus group. This should take approximately 45 minutes and will be recorded and transcribed. The aim of the focus groups is to raise the issues that youth workers might experience when being socialised into their first posts. I will be facilitating the group, asking questions relating to your first post experiences. Please feel free not to respond if you do not wish to answer certain questions. You may withdraw from the study at any time without giving your reasons.

Your answers and comments will be quoted as required within the dissertation. Your identity will not be disclosed. Where your words are quoted, you will remain anonymous and your group will be given a code, i.e. F1 or F2. All other details relating to your gender, first post and current post (if applicable) will not be transcribed. The tape recordings and transcriptions will be stored in a locked filing cabinet that will only be accessed by me.

I will be following the British Sociological Associations Code of Ethics during the course of the research.

The research will enable CYM to better prepare graduating students for their future employment. This will help graduates with the choices they make about future jobs and hopefully ensure a smooth transition into the professional workplace.

I have read the above information and agree to these conditions.

Signed

Print Name

Date

APPENDIX TWO
Letter of Informed Consent: Interviews

School of Sport and Education

Brunel University

Home address: 4 Broad Green Steeple Bumpstead, Suffolk CB9 7BW

Tel: 07732041998

Email:jfg33@cam.ac.uk

Thank you for agreeing to participate in this research.

This research is being conducted for a dissertation as part of an MA in Youth & Community studies at Brunel University. The dissertation topic is the professional socialisation of graduating youth workers into full time employment. I will be conducting a case study with participants who graduated from CYM Cambridge. The aim of the study is to find out what the professional socialisation issues are for graduating youth workers and how CYM can better prepare students for these issues.

The data will be collected using 2 focus groups, questionnaires and semi-structured interviews. You are invited to take part in a semi-structured interview. This should take approximately 45 minutes and will be recorded and transcribed. The aim of the interview is to find out about your experiences of work when you started your first post. Please feel free not to respond if you do not wish to answer certain questions. You may withdraw from the study at any time without giving your reasons.

Your answers and comments will be quoted as required within the dissertation. Your identity will not be disclosed. Where your words are quoted, you will remain anonymous. A code will be assigned to you, for example, A or B or C etc. All other details relating to your gender, first post and current post (if applicable) will not be transcribed. The tape recordings and transcriptions will be stored in a locked filing cabinet that will only be accessed by me.

I will be following the British Sociological Associations Code of Ethics during the course of the research.

The research will enable CYM to better prepare graduating students for their future employment. This will help graduates with the choices they make about future jobs and hopefully ensure a smooth transition into the professional workplace.

I have read the above information and agree to these conditions.

Signed
Print Name
Date

APPENDIX THREE

Letter of Informed Consent: Questionnaires

School of Sport and Education

Brunel University

Home address: 4 Broad Green Steeple Bumpstead, Suffolk CB9 7BW

Tel: 07732041998

Email:jfg33@cam.ac.uk

Thank you for agreeing to participate in this research.

This research is being conducted for a dissertation as part of an MA in Youth & Community studies at Brunel University. The dissertation topic is the professional socialisation of graduating youth workers into full time employment. I will be conducting a case study with participants who graduated from CYM Cambridge. The aim of the study is to find out what the professional socialisation issues are for graduating youth workers and how CYM can better prepare students for these issues.

The data will be collected using 2 focus groups, questionnaires and semi-structured interviews. You are invited to complete a questionnaire. This should take approximately 30 minutes. The aim of the questionnaire is to find out what issues you faced when you started your first post and to find out what responsibilities you had. Once you have completed the questionnaire please email it back to me. Please feel free not to respond if you do not wish to answer certain questions. You may withdraw from the study at any time without giving your reasons.

Your answers and comments will be quoted as required within the dissertation. Your identity will not be disclosed. Where your words are quoted, you will remain anonymous. A code will be assigned to your questionnaire, i.e. S01, S02 and so on. All other details relating to your gender, first post and current post (if applicable) will remain confidential. The questionnaires will be stored on my laptop, which is accessible by me with the use of a password.

I will be following the British Sociological Associations Code of Ethics during the course of the research

The research will enable CYM to better prepare graduating students for their future employment. This will help graduates with the choices they make about future jobs and hopefully ensure a smooth transition into the professional workplace.

I have read the above information and agree to these conditions.

Signed

Print Name

Date

APPENDIX FOUR

Interview Categories Based on Questionnaires

1) Describe why you first came on the course?

   a) Progression from voluntary work

   b) Develop experience

   c) To learn

   d) Called by God / youth ministry / theology

   e) For professional qualification and degree

   f) Could work and study at the same time

   g) To eventually be employed as a professional youth worker

   h) Passionate about Christian youth work

2) Describe your main placement responsibilities

   a) Co-ordinating youth programmes

   b) Developing volunteers

c) Managing volunteers

d) Developing young leaders

e) Running youth programmes

f) Detached work

g) Build relationships

h) Developing youth work

i) Partnership work

j) Discipleship of young people

k) Residentials

l) Outreach work

m) Schools work

RELATING TO FIRST POST

3) What was your first post upon graduating?

    a) Senior church youth worker

    b) Full time youth worker with youth service

    c) Church youth worker

    d) Drugs worker for local authority

    e) Drugs worker for secular charity

    f) Project co-ordinator for detached project

    g) Youth and Community worker for a church

4) Describe your first post responsibilities

    a) Establish the youth work for church and community

    b) Run youth work programmes

    c) Management of projects

    d) Management of volunteers/part time staff

e) Management of buildings

f) Management of resources

g) Partnership working

h) Advice on issues affecting young people

i) Discipleship of young people

j) Outreach

k) Schools work

l) Empowerment of young people

m) Co-ordinate youth work

n) Work ecumenically

o) Lead youth orientated youth services on Sundays

p) Provide in-house training

q) Run residentials

r) Develop youth provision

s) Apply for funding

t) Build links with local community

u) Deliver drugs information to young people

v) Pastoral work with young people

w) Group work

x) Detached work

y) Administration

5) Did the reflective practice method of learning benefit you in your first post?

   a) Continued learning through reading books

   b) Theories learnt were put into practice

   c) Mixture of practical and theoretical experience had significant impact

d) It became the 'norm' / second nature

e) I continue to use it with my staff

f) Informed my practice even in a different setting

g) Reflective skills continue to develop

h) Brought a reflective edge to the work that had been lacking

i) Work developed because of it

j) Helped in managing staff

k) Helped in decision making

6) Briefly describe your feelings during the first few weeks of your first post

    a) Relief having finished the course

    b) Lost

    c) Doubted abilities

    d) Anxiety about leaving support networks that were established

    e) Anxiety about making new friends

    f) Selfish for moving family

    g) Fear of the unknown

    h) Unconfident

    i) Energised

    j) Bewildered

    k) Nervous about new organisation and it's structures

    l) Learning a new professional 'language'

    m) Eager to start

    n) Freedom - to develop the work

    o) Sense of direction

p) Isolated

q) Unnerving going from working in a Christian setting to a secular post

r) Pleased to be paid

s) Confident in own ability

t) Exhausted – due to full time work and family

u) Scared at amount of trust being shown

v) Overwhelmed

7) Where there particular problems to overcome?

a) Terrible management

b) Difference in values

c) Difference in direction

d) Winning over staff after previous popular manager

e) Too much reading of policies

f) Too many other staff to get to know

g) Understanding the ethos and working of a different church denomination

h) Secular partners suspicious of Church work and hidden agendas

i) Church were suspicious of secular agencies

j) Parents concerned that youth work was beginning to work with 'wrong' type of young people

k) Funding bids

l) Gaining trust from new young people

m) Missing old placement

n) Multi-agency meetings were scary

o) Taking on board lots of new information

p) Getting used to full time work and impact on family

8) Did the course prepare you for your first post and the issues you faced?

  a) Developed assertiveness
  b) Knew purpose of youth work
  c) Developed confidence
  d) Apply new skills
  e) Learnt principles behind skill base
  f) Mostly yes, but placement didn't provide a wide enough work experience
  g) Provided good foundations for youth work
  h) Course did not prepare me for 'ministry' and a wife/mother

9) Did you experience any gaps in knowledge when you started your first post?

  a) Funding applications
  b) Workings of local authorities
  c) Basic first aid
  d) Secular professional language
  e) Government policy/initiatives
  f) Statutory sector bureaucracy
  g) Budgeting
  h) Partnership work
  i) What it meant being Christian in a secular organisation
  j) Accreditation
  k) Strategic thinking

l) How to work in partnership with a church and local authority

10) What were the expectations from your first employer?

    a) vague

    b) low as employer did not understand my level of training

    c) Manage staff

    d) Deliver relevant youth service within a tight budget

    e) Develop the work

    f) Group work facilitation

    g) One to one work

    h) Deliver quality youth work

11) Did you meet expectations?

    a) yes, until values differed

    b) Problem was in challenging what a youth worker was capable of

    c) Yes, but very stressed in trying to meet all expectations of a huge job

    d) Yes, but time and resources were tight

    e) Yes, but overwhelmed at times

    f) Yes, but had to work out expectations

12) Were there any support structures in your first post?

    a) Not really – support from friends and co students from the course

b) Had already developed mentor and pastoral support during placement and maintained this (most participants spoke of this)

c) Line manager

d) Spiritual director – set up after course finished

e) Non managerial supervision

f) Field work tutor from the course

g) Prayer partner

h) Local Christian youth workers network

13) Did you miss any aspect of the course once you graduated?

a) Journals

b) Continual learning

c) Academic environment

d) Support of tutors

e) Support/friendship of other students

f) No, that chapter finished

g) Placement/work ethos

h) In-depth conversations, theological and youth work practice

i) Co-workers

j) Young people

k) The challenging

l) Reflective time

APPENDIX FIVE

Data Analysis Categories

<u>Feelings of Post Graduates in First Post</u>

a) Enthusiastic

b) Overwhelmed by amount of responsibility and trust

c) Lonely / isolated

d) Missed the course, friends, tutors, family

e) Massive culture shock – new place

f) Anxious about decision making

g) Nervous about responsibility

h) Pressure of wanting to perform well / impress employer

i) Out of my depth

j) Worried due to being younger than those I managed

k) Confident

l) Relief having finished course

m) Independent – now getting paid

n) Excited, new lease of life

o) Anger, been set up to feel confident by course, but didn't know what I was doing

p) Intimidated by other professionals

q) Spiritually immature

r) Fake

s) Bewildered

t) Unconfident

u) Confused by new language

v) Self-doubt

w) Exhausted

x) Unsure if I would 'fit in'

Issues to Overcome During First Post

a) Understanding a different organisation

b) Understanding language being used

c) Partnership work and suspicions about hidden agendas

d) Building relationships with staff and young people

e) Management issues

f) Attitudes of fellow workers and suitability

Impact of Course on Post Graduates

a) Journal writing very positive impact

b) Understanding young people and youth work

c) Provided tools to work with young people

d) Taught to think

e) Reflective practitioner

f) Professionalism to take into church

g) Equipped for future role

h) Developed self-awareness

i) Broadened theoretical and practical knowledge

j) Can articulate my thoughts

k) Dissertation helped to get my first job

l) Confidence in own abilities

m) Enhanced passion for theology and young people

n) Self-management

o) Informed in entering first post

p) Encouraged further post grad education

q) Developed inter-relational skills

r) Transferable skills

Tension Between Training and First Post

a) Different sort of youth work

b) Differences in secular and Christian work

c) Low expectations of professional standard of new organisation (from graduate)

d) Employer lack of understanding of youth work role

e) Low expectations of youth work role coming from employer

f) High level of management tasks and high levels of face to face work

g) Difference in values

h) Too much management responsibility without the experience

i) Large, slow moving organisation – frustrating

j) Had to deconstruct learning and build up within a new environment

k) Huge organisation, so much to learn

l) Boundaries different due to nature of young people

Beliefs and Choice of First Post

a) Motivation to do course, to be a Christian in a secular world

b) As a young person realised wanted to work with under-privileged young people

c) 'Called'

d) Sharing lives with young people

e) Personal theology developed through course

f) Faith challenged by course

g) Christian journey

Gaps in Knowledge

a) Government policy changes were happening as I graduated, Transforming Youth work etc

b) Lack of knowledge about organisational practices

c) Management

d) Strategic thinking

e) Accreditation for young people

f) Structure of organisation

g) Budgeting, fund raising

h) Partnership working

i) What is meant being Christian in a secular post

j) Language

Support Structures

a) Field work tutors

b) Professional Formation groups

c) Placement

d) Fellow students

e) Family

f) Friends

g) Tutors

h) Pastor from voluntary days

i) Non-managerial support – once in new post

j) Line manager

k) Spiritual Director

l) Pastoral support

m) Work colleagues

APPENDIX SIX
Questionnaire

This questionnaire is about finding out what your experience were when you started your first post after graduating from CYM. I would also like to hear about your specific responsibilities.

1. Age on graduating from CYM

2. What year did you graduate?

3. Briefly describe why you wanted to do the course initially

4. Did you graduate with JNC?

5. What was your first job upon graduating from the course?

6.   Was the organisation Christian or secular?

7.   Please describe your main responsibilities

8.   What modules/aspects from the course had been particularly helpful when you undertook your first post?

9.   What modules/aspects were not so helpful?

10. When you were training did you find the combination of theory and practice a useful method for learning? Please explain your answer

11. Did this method of learning benefit you in your first post? Please explain

12. When you began in your first post after graduating, briefly describe your feelings during the first few weeks

13. Were there particular problems that you had to overcome? Please explain your answer

14. Did the course prepare you for your first post and the issues you faced? Please explain

15. Did you experience any gaps in your knowledge when you started your first post? Please explain

16. Were there any support systems (i.e. non-managerial, pastoral or others) in place in your first post that you found particularly helpful? Please explain

17. What were the expectations on you from your first employer?

18. Did you feel able to meet these expectations? Please explain

19. Did you miss any aspect of being on the course once you graduated? Please explain

Thank you for completing this questionnaire!
Please return by email

APPENDIX SEVEN

Semi-Structured Interview:

Guide Questions

Turn on the Dictaphone

Thank the participant

Provide an overview of the research

1.   Where was your first post?

2.   What responsibilities did you have?

3.   What feelings did you have when you first started?

4.   Were there any particular issues that you had to overcome?

5.   Have you noticed any changes in your practice since
         leaving the course?

6.   Did you miss anything about the course when you left?

Thank the participant again at the end

APPENDIX EIGHT

Focus Group: Guide Questions

Turn on Dictaphone

Thank the group

Review the research and explain role within the group

1.   When you left the course, did you feel prepared to begin your first posts?

2.   What sort of posts did you enter?

3.   How did you feel in the first few weeks?

4.   Were there any particular issues to overcome?

5.   Did you feel equipped to deal with these issues?

6.   Did you miss any aspect of the course when you left?

Thank the participants again for their time